THE MYSTERY OF...

THE
PYRAMIDS

BY
HARRIETTE ABELS

EDITED BY
Dr. Howard Schroeder
Professor in Reading and Language Arts
Dept. of Curriculum and Instruction
Mankato State University

PUBLISHED BY
CRESTWOOD HOUSE

CIP

LIBRARY OF CONGRESS CATALOGING IN PUBLICATION DATA

Abels, Harriette Sheffer.
 Pyramids.

 (The Mystery of ——)
 SUMMARY: Examines the various mysteries of the Great Pyramid of Cheops,
discussing its design and construction in ancient Egypt and if predictions about the
future and confirmations of truths from the Bible can be found within its walls.
 1. Great Pyramid (Egypt)—Juvenile literature. 2. Pyramids—Juvenile literature.
3 Egypt—Antiquities—Juvenile literature. [1. Great Pyramid (Egypt) 2. Pyramids.
3. Egypt—Antiquities] I. Schroeder, Howard. II. Title. III. Series.
DT63.A24   1987   932   87-15455
ISBN 0-89686-345-X

International Standard Book Number:	Library of Congress Catalog Card Number:
0-89686-345-X	87-15455

CREDITS

Illustrations:
Cover Photo: UPI/Bettmann Newsphotos
Egyptian Tourist Authority: 5, 13, 44-45
AP/Wide World Photos: 6-7, 21
Mary Evans Picture Library: 10, 22-23, 30
Bob Williams: 14-15, 16-17, 19, 24-25, 33, 37, 40-41
UPI/Bettmann Newsphotos: 27, 28-29, 34-35, 39
J.R. Beebe/Egyptian Tourist Authority: 42-43
Andy Schlabach: 46
Graphic Design & Production:
Baker Street Productions, Ltd.

CRESTWOOD HOUSE

Box 3427, Mankato, MN, U.S.A. 56002

THE PYRAMIDS

TABLE OF CONTENTS

Chapter 1

It is nightfall in Egypt. On the sandy plains of Giza, across from the Nile River, stands the city of Cairo. Lights start flickering on, one at a time. The city settles into its evening rhythms.

Ten miles away, ancient stone monuments keep a rhythm all their own. They jut upwards from the earth, and seem to touch the night sky with their huge peaks. In the air is a sense of ancient wonder and accomplishment.

These are the pyramids of Egypt—one of the greatest mysteries of all time.

The most famous of these stone monuments is the Great Pyramid of Cheops. Cheops was the king of Egypt around 2600 B.C. Cheops is the Greek version of his name. In Egyptian he was called Khufu.

Although the Great Pyramid is known as the burial place of this king, his body has never been found. However, several writings with his name were found on the ceiling slabs above the "King's Chamber" in the pyramid. This is why archaeologists believe that there was some connection between Cheops and the pyramid.

The Great Pyramid sits on a plateau ten miles (16

The pyramids of Egypt are an age-old mystery.

km) west of the city of Cairo in the Nile River Valley. There are two other pyramids close by, slightly smaller in size. Smaller yet are the six pyramids believed to have been built for Cheops' wives and daughters.

About twelve hundred feet (366 m) southeast of the Great Pyramid is a stone monument that is known as the Great Sphinx. It looks like a human head on the body of a lion. The Sphinx was carved from a single sandstone knoll. It is two hundred forty feet (73 m) long, sixty-six feet (20 m) high and thirteen feet and eight inches (4 m) at its widest point. On the head is carved an ancient Egyptian headdress. A cobra is carved on its forehead. These are said to be ancient symbols of Egyptian royalty. No one knows why this strange statue

The half-man, half-lion Sphinx seems to stand guard over the pyramids.

was built.

Some scientists think the Sphinx may once have been covered with plaster and painted in bright colors. However, the Sphinx has been badly damaged by the blowing sands of the desert. Today, it is just bare sand-

stone, with no traces of paint left.

There are about one hundred other pyramids along the western bank of the Nile River. It is believed that the oldest pyramid is the "stepped" pyramid of Saqqarah. It was built for King Zoser about 2650 B.C. by a famous Egyptian architect named Imhotep. Instead of smooth sides, stepped pyramids have outer steps, or terraces, that can be climbed. Some stepped pyramids were later changed into smooth pyramids.

But it is the Great Pyramid of Cheops that is most interesting to scientists. They think it was built some time after 2600 B.C. It is the only pyramid that has a square base and is built entirely of stone. It has more than two million stone blocks that weigh about two and a half tons (2.3 MT) each.

An ancient tale says that the pyramid is connected by tunnels to other pyramids, to the Sphinx, and to small temples and other buildings. If the story is true, these have long since disappeared. But some scientists believe that the pyramid still has undiscovered rooms.

In 1839, workers were clearing out the passages of the sealed-up pyramid. A strong, cold wind suddenly began to blow through the passages. It was so strong that for two days the men had trouble keeping their lamps lit. Then the wind stopped as suddenly as it had started. No one has ever learned where it came from.

A man working in the same area in the 1950's heard strange noises in the pyramid. He, too, felt that there must be undiscovered passageways, either inside or underneath the pyramid.

Chapter 2

What is the Great Pyramid? For a thousand years people have been trying to learn its true purpose. Some scientists tell us that it is an almanac that contains facts and figures about the heavens. With it, the length of the year can be measured. This can be done as accurately as with a modern telescope. The pyramid is also a compass for telling directions. It is so accurate that modern compasses are adjusted to it. The position of the pyramid, and the stones that form it, give scientists these accurate measurements.

The pyramid was also an important landmark to the ancient world. It may have been used as an observatory from which maps and tables were drawn. In its sides and angles is a ''map'' of the northern hemisphere. In fact, it is a correct-scale model of the hemisphere. It shows the geographical degrees of latitude (east and west measurements of the earth) and longitude (north and south measurements).

In 1853, it was discovered that the Great Pyramid also works as a large sundial. This led to the theory that the pyramid builders had meant for their structure to serve as a perfect almanac to mark the passing of the seasons and the years.

Workers explore a chamber in the Great Pyramid.

10

There are some people who believe that the Great Pyramid contains a coded history of the human race. They say that this code shows us not only history, but also the future. These people find support for their theory in every measurement made on the giant structure. They read it like a road map. Every block, crack, and angle has been measured and added to their theory.

Another theory is that the pyramid was built as an observatory. The tops of most of the pyramids are usually small, flat surfaces that would be ideal for gazing at the heavens. This would account for the absence of a capstone. If a capstone had been placed on the structure, there would have been no place to stand.

One theory is that the pyramid was simply a landmark, used as a road marker so that travelers could see it as they crossed the desert. But most archaeologists agree that it is much too complex a structure for that.

Chapter 3

No one knows who built the Great Pyramid or how it was done. The builders left no records of their methods. It is very odd that there are no writings about how the work was done, as the Egyptians usually kept detailed records of everything that happened in their civilization.

Most scientists believe that construction on the Great Pyramid started in 2644 B.C. Others believe that it was not begun until 2200 B.C., taking up to fifty-six years to complete. Still others think that the pyramid is at least a thousand years older. We may never know for sure.

Today, the Great Pyramid does not look as it did when it was built. Over the centuries its height has eroded from 481 feet (147 m) to 450 feet (137 m) tall. It sits on about thirteen acres (5 hectares), and each side is about 756 feet (230 m) in length. The four sides lean at an angle of about 51 degrees and 52 minutes to the ground.

The Great Pyramid is called a true pyramid. It has a perfect square for a base. Each of its four sides is an equilateral triangle (having sides equal in length). The four sides meet at a point that is directly above the center of the base.

How were the pyramids built? We may never know for sure.

Shown above is an artist's conception of the construction site of the Great Pyramid.

14

The building of the Great Pyramid was so difficult that, even today, there are many different theories as to how it was done. However, scientists agree about some of the methods that must have been used.

The first thing that had to be done was to clear the Giza plateau. This was done by removing the loose sand and gravel and digging down to bedrock. The plateau was then leveled out and the ruts and holes filled in. Recent testing has shown that the base rock is less than one inch (2.5 cm) off level.

The next step was to lay a row of white rectangular

Lifting the heavy stones into place must have been hard work!

limestone slabs as a pavement. After that came the most critical step: drawing the first straight side. This must have been done by watching the rising and setting of certain stars, over and over.

Large limestone corner blocks were then set into the rock base. They formed the square corners for the first rows of casing stones. The joints between the stones can barely be seen. There are twenty-two acres (9 hectares) of these casing stones. Engineers are puzzled as to how the heavy stones were raised and put into place.

The outside of the pyramid was covered with thick slabs of white limestone. Archaeologists think that most of the limestone blocks were brought from quarries a few miles across the Nile, on the Arabian side of the river. Some of the blocks, however, may have come from the Giza hills.

Recently, a chemist at a university in Florida has come up with a different idea. Joseph Davidovits believes the blocks are not solid rock from a quarry. He thinks they are a type of molded concrete. According to his theory, every stone was cast exactly where we see it today. The edge of a finished stone was used as part of the mold for the next stone.

The samples that Davidovits took from the Egyptian quarries were almost pure limestone. But he says the stones in the pyramids are limestone and rock rubble. These are bound together with a cement made of minerals common in the Nile area.

If this latest theory is true, we now have the answer as to how the stones were put in place. They weren't! They were made right on the site as they were needed.

The builders of the pyramids may have used limestone from across the Nile River. According to some historians, they probably moved the heavy load using rowboats and a huge barge.

19

Chapter 4

Who built the Great Pyramid? The most common belief is that the Egyptians did. But it's possible that the pyramid may not have been built by Egyptians at all. Some scientists think that a small band of colonists, either from Asia or the Euphrates River area, were the real builders. They must have had very advanced scientific and mathematical knowledge. Once they had built the pyramid, they left Egypt without ever telling their hosts how they had managed the great feat. This would explain the lack of Egyptian writings on the subject.

One scientist thinks that the plans for building the Great Pyramid were drawn up long before the actual structure was built. He also believes that it was the design of one person. This person must have come from an unknown civilization that was far ahead of the rest of the world in scientific and cultural achievements.

The Arabs have a tradition that the pyramids were built shortly before a worldwide flood by a king who had a vision. He thought that the world was going to turn upside down and the stars would fall from the heavens. The king decided to put all the wisdom he had into the pyramids. This included the secrets of astronomy, physics and geometry. According to the

The pyramid of Cheops is the last of the "seven ancient wonders of the world."

legend, the Great Pyramid predicts the position of the stars and the cycles of the heavenly bodies.

Mystics in the past and modern times have been fascinated with the pyramids. Many of these people believe that there was once a great order of mystics. These people understood astronomy, mathematics and construction. They built their knowledge not only into the Great Pyramid, but also into the important temples of other great civilizations.

Many stone structures from ancient cultures still exist. However, we have very little knowledge about the people themselves. In South America there is a build-

The illustration above shows the pyramids at Mastaba, Egypt. Note how closely the stones fit together.

ing formed by stones of irregular cuts. They fit together exactly. Some of these stones are as much as twenty times larger than the stones of the Great Pyramid—yet they were wedged into place in perfect lines.

In Peru there is a great wall thought to have been built by an ancient Indian tribe. It is sixty feet (18 m) high and almost a half mile (.8 km) long. There is a stone in the wall that is ten feet (3 m) wide, seventeen feet (5 m) high, and nine feet (2.7 m) thick. It weighs over one hundred tons (90 MT). No mortar was used in building this wall. The stones are interlocked so perfectly that even a major earthquake could not shake it.

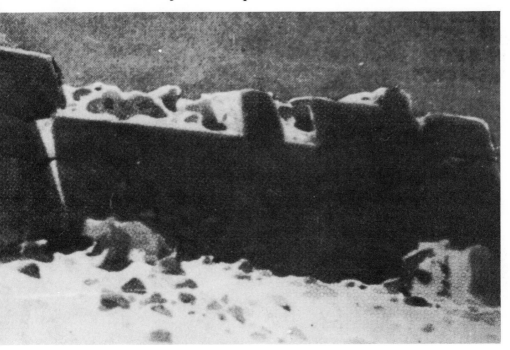

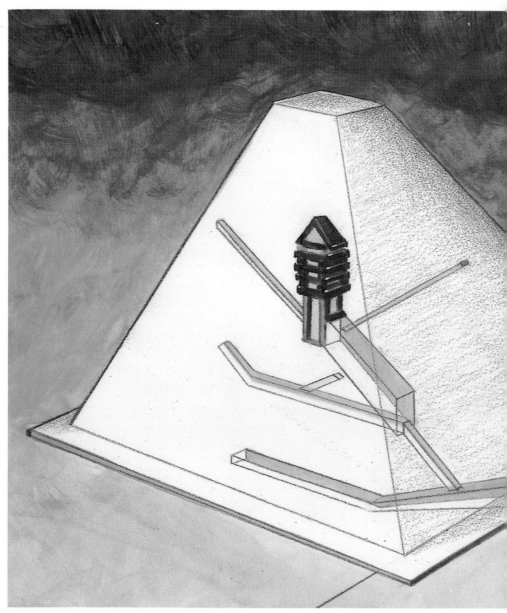

The builders of the pyramids must have had advanced scientific and mathematical knowledge.

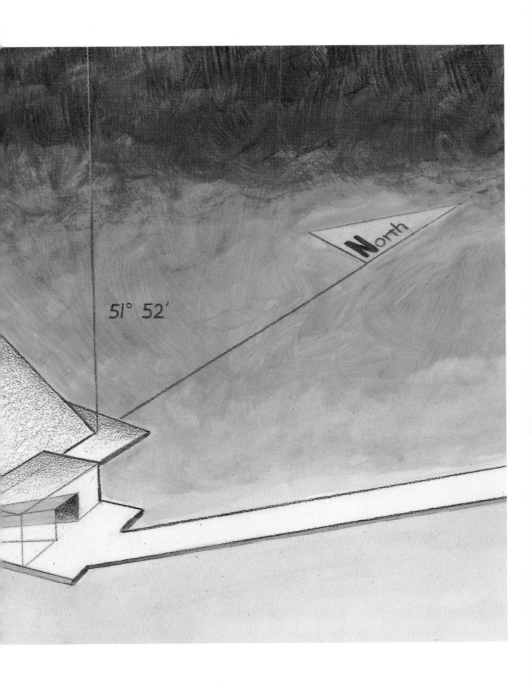

51° 52′

North

Chapter 5

Edgar Cayce was a famous American psychic known as the Sleeping Prophet. In his psychic readings, he gave a much earlier date for the Great Pyramid and the Sphinx. He said they dated back to 10,000 B.C. He also said that there are cultural similarities between Egypt and Yucatan (an area in southeast Mexico and northern Central America). Both of these cultures have pyramids, Cayce said, because people migrated to both lands when the continent of Atlantis sank into the ocean.

In his readings, Cayce first described prehistoric Egypt. The study of the spiritual nature of man began by carving spiritual laws on tablets of stone and slate. Cayce called this the first Bible.

About three hundred years before Atlantis disappeared, he said, a large group of people in eastern Europe were given a prophecy by a young priest. This priest said that an Arabian tribe would march to Egypt and make it a better place for both races. Egypt would then become the leading nation of that time. The young priest's prediction came true, according to Cayce. The king of this tribe led an expedition to Egypt and became the founder of the first Egyptian Dynasty.

Word of the wonderful new Egyptian civilization

Pyramids similar to those of Egypt have been found in other cultures. Shown above is the Pyramid of the Sun in Veracruz, Mexico.

27

spread to other continents. Wise men came from other countries to see and learn about the wonderful things these people could do. According to Cayce, some of the countries they came from were India, Peru, Norway, Mongolia, and China.

Some people felt that the wisdom of this great Egyptian culture should be kept in a safe place for the benefit of future generations. The site selected was the fertile plain of Giza. It was thought of as the center of the earth. Therefore, there would be fewer problems with future

Will shifting desert sands uncover another pyramid?

earthquakes or floods. The records were to be hidden in a small pyramid between the Sphinx and the Great Pyramid. Underground tunnels would connect all three monuments.

Cayce said that hidden in the northeast corner of this small pyramid, thirty-two stone tablets are buried with the remains of an ancient king. This was the first of the pyramids to be built. Cayce believes that someday it will be uncovered by the shifting of the desert sands.

It took one hundred years to build the Great Pyramid,

Cayce revealed. It was meant to be a ceremonial hall for those who wished to dedicate themselves to the religion of Egypt.

According to Cayce, the pyramid once had a cap-stone. It was made of a mixture of copper, brass and

Cayce believed that the chambers and passageways of the pyramids held the story of the spiritual development of man.

gold. In certain seasons, a fire was lighted for religious purposes.

In the smaller pyramid of records, the one that has not yet been found, there is a vault sealed with heavy metal containing the prophecies for the period from 1958 to 1998.

Cayce believes that the length, breadth, height and direction of the many layers of stone in the passages and chambers report the events of importance in the spiritual development of man. He said the birth and death of Jesus of Nazareth are clearly shown to the year, day and hour at the turn of the passageway leading to the queen's chamber.

The pyramid prophesied 1936 as a year of great disorder, with wars, storms and land upheavals, followed by great unrest among people, Cayce said. He gave his reading ten years earlier, and could not possibly have known that by 1936 the forces that would lead to World War II were already in motion.

He saw a time of adjustment coming by 1956, with great advancements in science and medicine. The end of this "era of preparation" would come in 1998. Cayce predicted that the year 2000 A.D. would be the beginning of the so-called "Golden Age of Man."

Other people have also "read" the predictions believed to be built into the pyramids. Some of these predictions are the same as Cayce's, while others are very different. There are many people who believe that the Great Pyramid holds the secrets of the future world.

Chapter 6

Some people believe that the very shape of the pyramid has "magical" powers. In earlier times this belief was only passed around by word of mouth. Today, there are many books written on the subject.

In the early 1930's, several men "rediscovered" the ability of the pyramid shape to affect matter. They were laughed at by other scientists, but continued their research in spite of that.

The new interest in the study of pyramid energy came about when a Frenchman, Antoine Bovis, was on vacation in Egypt in the 1930's. As a tourist, Bovis went to visit the Great Pyramid. In one of the chambers he found the bodies of small animals that had wandered into the pyramid. They had lost their way and starved to death. What startled Mr. Bovis was that the flesh of the animals had not rotted away! Instead, the creatures had simply dehydrated or mummified.

Bovis was very interested. When he returned to France, he built his own three-foot (91 cm) wooden pyramid. It was made to the exact proportions of the Great Pyramid. To his surprise, Bovis found that his small pyramid could copy the mummification process of the Great Pyramid. He also found he could preserve

The shape of the pyramid may prevent bodies from decaying. Shown above is a "mummy."

One man believed so much in the power of pyramids that he built this house in Gurnee, Illinois.

fruits and vegetables in it. Bovis now believed that a strange energy was at work within the pyramid. He wrote several short articles and gave many talks on his discovery.

Very few people believed Bovis' work. But there were some people who read about it and continued the experiments on their own. A doctor in Stockholm, Sweden, experimented with the effect of water on steel. He found that the pyramid shape stopped rust from forming. It allowed the metal to retain its hardness.

It does not seem to matter whether a pyramid is made out of cloth, metal, glass or wood. The results are the same. A clear plastic pyramid, however, is harmful to humans. The National Aeronautics and Space Administration (NASA) has found that plastics on a spacecraft absorb and block the passage of negative ions (atoms that carry an electric charge). This is important to the crews' health and mental state.

Pyramids have been used to improve the health of everything from tropical fish to houseplants. Some people feel that pyramids help them sleep better at night. Others believe they give people more energy and better health.

People who sleep under a pyramid frame have reported many different feelings. Some say their dreams are more clear and colorful. Others report that they wake up feeling better rested and are more alert during the day. One person said it felt as if he had been sleeping on a mountain top.

Not all of these feelings have been pleasant. Some people have reported a ringing in their ears. Others say that the top of their head gets very warm. Still others feel cold all over.

Pyramids have also been used to improve the flavor of foods. Meat and other foods have been mummified. Some experiments have aged wine by using the pyramid shape. There have been reports that it has increased the life span of small animals. And many of the experiments had to do with the growth rate of plants.

As with most experiments, the results are not always the same. But positive results are seen most often when the pyramid is lined up correctly with the earth's magnetic fields.

Some people claim that sleeping under a pyramid frame gives them more energy and better health.

Chapter 7

In the 1970's, pyramids became quite a fad. Many wild claims were made for the power of pyramid energy, and "Pyramid Power" became an everyday phrase. A lot of the claims turned out to be untrue. But some of the experiments seemed to work. It is possible to do simple experiments with pyramid power right in your own home.

Models of pyramids can be made out of different materials. Glass, cardboard, wood, copper, concrete, and aluminum are all good materials. But the pyramid should be built according to the mathematics of the Great Pyramid. Before building a pyramid, it is best to use a compass and establish true north. One side must face in that direction.

Another important thing to remember is that a pyramid must be free from metal pipes and other objects that could interfere with the Earth's magnetic fields. Some people believe that to get the best results, the object tested should be placed a third of the way up from the base of the pyramid. This area is the "point of balance" of a pyramid. Place the food, flower or whatever you want to experiment with on a small platform.

*For a while, pyramids were quite a fad! In 1981, this "pyramid" com-
peted for the title of Best-Dressed Pyramid in a contest in London,
England.*

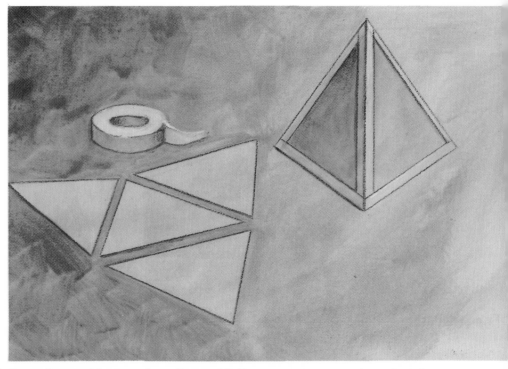

Does "pyramid power" really work? Try your own experiment and find out!

A very simple, basic pyramid can be made out of cardboard and tape. Make four identical triangles. Now tape the four sides together in an upright position. With a compass, find the exact location of magnetic north. Place the pyramid so that one of the four sides faces directly north. Your experiment can be done on anything—fruit, vegetables or even small insects. If you are going to experiment with food, it is best to cut a

few holes in the side of the pyramid so air can get in. If the pyramid is properly placed, the food should dehydrate without spoiling.

Some experiments have been done with pyramids and minerals. Topaz, quartz, amethyst and clear rock crystal were used. The minerals gave off a very definite heat. Sometimes there seemed to be a pulsing vibration that came from the tips of the rocks. The clear quartz, called rock crystal, was the most powerful of the minerals. This is the crystal that so-called fortune-tellers use in their "crystal balls."

It is said that in ancient Egypt, priests would place a piece of clear rock crystal on their forehead. They said this gave them psychic visions and helped them in their work as healers. Perhaps this is another one

The Great Pyramid in Giza holds many ancient secrets.

of the ancient secrets hidden in the Great Pyramid in Giza.

We shall probably never know much about the ancient people who built this marvelous structure. We won't know what it was used for, or how it was built. But one thing seems clear: We will continue to enjoy the powerful, age-old beauty of the pyramids. And we will keep on wondering.

*People will always be fascinated by the beauty and mystery of the
pyramids.*

44

Map

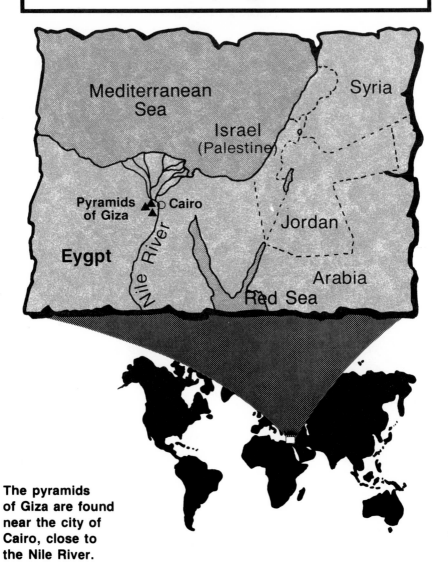

The pyramids
of Giza are found
near the city of
Cairo, close to
the Nile River.

Glossary/Index